GROUNDBREAKERS
RULE-BREAKERS
& REBELS

50 UNSTOPPABLE
ST. LOUIS WOMEN

BY KATIE J. MOON / ILLUSTRATIONS BY RORI!

MISSOURI HISTORICAL SOCIETY PRESS

ST. LOUIS, MISSOURI

DISTRIBUTED BY UNIVERSITY OF CHICAGO PRESS

**To the women of St. Louis—
your strength and resilience
inspire me every day.**

Library of Congress Cataloging-in-Publication Data

Names: Moon, Katie J., 1977- author. | Rori!, 1978- illustrator.
Title: Groundbreakers, rule-breakers & rebels : 50 unstoppable St. Louis
   women / Katie J. Moon ; illustrations by Rori!.
Other titles: Groundbreakers, rule-breakers and rebels
Description: St. Louis : Missouri Historical Society Press, 2020. |
   Includes index. | Summary: "The individual stories of 50 groundbreaking
   women from St. Louis, with original illustrations"-- Provided by
   publisher.
Identifiers: LCCN 2020022991 | ISBN 9781883982980 (paperback)
Subjects: LCSH: Women--Missouri--Saint Louis--Biography. |
   Reformers--Missouri--Saint Louis--Biography. | Social
   change--Missouri--Saint Louis--Anecdotes. | Saint Louis
   (Mo.)--Biography.
Classification: LCC F474.S253 A263 2020 | DDC 305.409778/66--dc23
LC record available at https://lccn.loc.gov/2020022991

Distributed by University of Chicago Press
Designed by Tom White
Printed and bound in the United States by Modern Litho

INTRODUCTION

The history of women's activism in St. Louis began long before 1920, when the 19th Amendment became US law and gave women the right to vote. Women have always been a fundamental–but often forgotten–part of St. Louis's past. By taking a closer look at St. Louis women's lives across generations, a clearer picture of the city's history begins to emerge. Gaining the right to vote was the culmination of the countless contributions and remarkable achievements by women of every race, class, and creed.

In this book, you'll discover not only the individual stories of groundbreaking women, but also stories of women working together to help create a better city. Every woman faced certain difficulties and restrictions simply because of her gender. The victories were hard won and well earned. But when women's focus turned toward suffrage–gaining the right to vote–they were unstoppable.

Although a major battle was won in 1920, when most women across the country gained the right to vote, St. Louis women from all walks of life still faced challenges of gender discrimination and inequality. The fight for equal rights wore on throughout the 20th century, and it continues today.

ARAMEPINCHIEUE (MARIE ROUENSA)

ca. 1677–1725

The fate of two nations hinged on one woman's decision to get married– and she was all too aware of the consequences it could bring. Marie, the 17-year-old daughter of Chief Rouensa of southern Illinois's Kaskaskia tribe, had recently converted to Catholicism and was deeply religious. In fact, she wanted to remain single and devote her life to the Church. When her father demanded that she marry Michel Accault, a disreputable French trader twice her age, she refused. She was kicked out of the house, and her father brought all religious services in the village to a halt.

Marie wasn't simply refusing to be married. She was refusing an opportunity to create a mutually beneficial partnership between members of the Kaskaskia tribe and French settlers. After much deliberation, she agreed to marry Michel, with the agreement that their children would be baptized as Catholics. Her motivation was twofold: She knew the economic advantages that would come with intermarriage, and she prayed that the marriage would encourage her parents' conversion to Catholicism as well as her future husband's return to the Church.

Marie and Michel married in 1694 and had two children. Both children were baptized, and her parents converted to Catholicism as she had hoped. When Michel passed away in 1703, Marie remarried, had six more children, and became a village leader. She remained devoted to her faith until her death in 1725. Even today she is the only woman to be buried under the floor of the Immaculate Conception Church in Kaskaskia–a sign of her respected status in the community.

MARIE THÉRÈSE BOURGEOIS CHOUTEAU

1733–1814

A strong woman with strong opinions, Marie Thérèse Bourgeois Chouteau used her power and influence to help transform a tiny fur-trading post into a flourishing city. Often considered the mother of St. Louis, Marie was the first European woman to reside in the new village at the invitation of its founder, Pierre Laclède. Her voyage to St. Louis was likely spurred by the decision to remove herself and her small children from an abusive marriage.

Born in New Orleans, Marie was married at 15 and soon gave birth to a son, only to be deserted by her husband, René Chouteau, a short time later. Although still legally married to René, she became romantically involved with Pierre Laclède and had four more children. Known throughout the village as Veuve (Widow) Chouteau, Marie never married Pierre–probably to protect herself from his growing debt. All five of her children kept the Chouteau surname, and none of them officially recognized Pierre as their biological father.

In her large stone home at the center of town, she maintained a bustling household, conducted business, hosted foreign dignitaries, and–like many of the city's wealthier residents–enslaved people. All of Marie's children married influential St. Louisans and had many children of their own, but Marie continued to make important financial and political decisions for the entire family (and the city) until her death in 1814.

ESTHER

1753–1833

When Esther was given to Jacques Clamorgan as payment for her enslaver's debt in 1784, her future seemed grim. Enslaved since birth, Esther would eventually be set free and become an astute businesswoman, wealthy property owner, and litigator who fought for herself and her family in court. But her life was not an easy one.

Soon after Jacques brought Esther to his home in St. Louis, she became his trusted housekeeper and business adviser. She managed his home, property, and slaves when he was out of town on business. In 1793 he freed Esther and gave her land—not out of goodwill, but as a way to hide his assets from the men he was indebted to. Esther continued to live with him, even though she now owned property.

Jacques later tried to force Esther to sign the property back to him, but she refused, and his physical abuse of her intensified. She left him, and despite not knowing how to read or write, she took the paperwork related to her land as well as her emancipation papers. The two fought over the properties in court until Esther's death in 1833, but she managed to hold on to a significant amount: an entire city block, two other city lots with houses, and approximately 100 acres of valuable farmland.

ANNA MARIA VON PHUL

1786–1823

What did early St. Louis and the people who lived here look like? It'd be much harder to know without Anna Maria von Phul's detailed sketches and paintings. Still unmarried at 32, Anna Maria probably began visiting her brother, Henry, in St. Louis hoping to find a suitor from his social circle. While she was here, she created art that endures as a rare visual record of colonial St. Louis.

Anna Maria attended finishing school in Lexington, Kentucky, where she took classes in watercolor and drawing, and by age 14 she had shown an aptitude for art. After her brother moved to St. Louis and her sister, Sarah, moved to nearby Edwardsville, she visited them frequently. She moved to St. Louis permanently in 1821, and with no household to manage or children to raise, Anna Maria spent her days sketching and painting. She drew houses, animals, and riverscapes, but she seemed most interested in capturing the well-dressed ladies, Creole boatmen, and Native Americans who made up St. Louis's diverse society.

Anna Maria died suddenly of a fever in 1823 at the age of 37, but the images she left behind are among the best remaining visual clues about everyday life in St. Louis decades before photography existed.

ST. ROSE PHILIPPINE DUCHESNE

1769–1852

When God calls, you answer, even at the age of 48. For Rose Philippine Duchesne, her decision to leave her religious community in Paris and begin a new life on the edge of the American frontier was an easy one. From an early age she dreamed that one day she would serve God among Native American children, and her dream finally seemed to be coming true.

Philippine traveled to St. Louis in 1818 with four companions–the first Catholic sisters to arrive–expecting to open a school in the city. But the plan had changed, and her school would now be established in the frontier outpost of St. Charles. Philippine was adept at navigating the power structure of the Catholic Church, and by 1827 she'd opened a school in St. Louis. Though there was a need to educate white students, she also welcomed Native Americans until their families were forced to move so far away that it was no longer viable. There was a special school for Black students one day a week, though they were taught in a segregated classroom. She eventually directed three schools, including the Academy of the Sacred Heart, which was the first free school west of the Mississippi and the first Catholic school in the region.

Philippine finally realized her childhood dream in 1841, at the age of 72, when she joined a mission to the Potawatomi tribe at Sugar Creek, Kansas. They named her *Quahkahkanumad*, One–Who–Prays–Always. Less than a year later, poor health forced her to return to St. Charles, where she lived until her death in 1852. She was canonized as a saint in 1988 by Pope John Paul II.

LIBERATOR

MARY MEACHUM

ca. 1801–1869

The threat of being arrested, jailed, or killed didn't stop Mary Meachum from working toward abolition. Born into slavery in Kentucky, Mary was brought to St. Louis by her enslaver in 1815. Her husband, John, purchased her freedom a short time later, and she dedicated the rest of her life to educating and freeing other enslaved persons.

Even after Missouri outlawed the education of all Black people–free and enslaved–the Meachums ran their school for African Americans. It's thought that they moved their school to a steamboat on the Mississippi River because Illinois "owned" the river's east side. If Missouri officials tried to apprehend anyone onboard, the boat could simply be moved into Illinois waters, where there were fewer restrictions on education.

When John died in 1854, Mary continued to use their home as a safe-house for the Underground Railroad. She was arrested in May 1855 for attempted "slave theft" when she was caught helping ferry enslaved persons to Illinois. The charges against her were eventually dropped. By 1864, Mary was the president of the Colored Ladies Soldiers' Aid Society, an organization formed in 1863 to assist the Black Union soldiers, refugees, and escaped slaves who were living at Benton Barracks during the Civil War.

HARRIET SCOTT

ca. 1815–1876

Although Missouri was a slave state, people were allowed to bring freedom suits: That is, men and women who could prove that they had been illegally enslaved could sue for their freedom. For women, being released from slavery also meant freedom for their children, and Harriet Robinson Scott desperately wanted her two daughters, Eliza and Lizzie, to be free.

Harriet was born into slavery in Virginia; a federal Indian agent took her to Fort Snelling in the Wisconsin territory in the early 1830s. Slavery was illegal there, but the US government looked the other way. Soon she met Dred Scott, an enslaved man, and they married in 1837. Harriet became the property of Dr. John Emerson, a military surgeon who also enslaved Dred. The couple moved with Dr. Emerson to Florida and then to St. Louis after he died, where his widow's family lived.

On April 6, 1846, Harriet and Dred filed separate freedom suit petitions, as both of them had lived in places where slavery was illegal. For the next 11 years, the Scotts waited for a final answer–but it wasn't the one they had hoped for. After their case had been reviewed by five different courts, the Scotts finally stood before the US Supreme Court and received the devastating news that their petition had been denied. In fact, the court ruled that as Black people, the Scotts would never be American citizens, and they would never enjoy the rights as stated in the Constitution.

Still, they persevered. Just two months after the Supreme Court decision, the Scott family was sold to the Blow family in St. Louis, who freed them immediately. But freedom was bittersweet for Harriet: Dred passed away just one year later.

EMILY PARSONS

1824–1880

During the Civil War nurses were required to be between the ages of 25 and 50 and in top mental and physical health. Emily Parsons was blind in one eye, deaf in one ear, and unable to stand for long periods of time because of a poorly healed ankle injury. But by 1863 she was a skilled surgical nurse at a St. Louis military hospital.

Emily went to nursing school in her hometown of Boston but knew her skills were needed closer to the war's front lines. She headed to St. Louis, then worked as the head nurse on a hospital steamboat for wounded soldiers. She contracted malaria but recovered and continued to work.

Despite her physical limitations, Emily's contributions to the war effort were invaluable. The doctor in charge of Benton Barracks, the largest military hospital in St. Louis, hired her to supervise all of the nurses there and to manage the treatment of more than 2,000 wounded soldiers. She lived at the barracks, caring full time for the soldiers and the growing number of African American refugees. After the war she returned to Boston, where she opened a charity hospital for women and children.

ELIZABETH KECKLY

1818–1907

In 1868, only one woman in the United States could write a book about her life called *Behind the Scenes: Or, Thirty Years a Slave, and Four Years in the White House.* That woman was Elizabeth Keckly (sometimes spelled Keckley). Born into slavery in Virginia in 1818, "Lizzy" was sold to a family that moved to St. Louis. Her new enslaver needed income and hired out Lizzy as a seamstress to the city's elite families. For two years her work supported a household of 17 people.

Lizzy eventually negotiated a deal with her enslaver to purchase her freedom for $1,200—about $35,000 today. Her wealthy clients loaned Lizzy the money she needed, and she worked in St. Louis for five more years to repay her benefactors.

Now free to relocate and open her own business, Lizzy moved to Washington, DC, in 1860, where her reputation as a skilled seamstress spread quickly. She was soon sewing dresses for the wives of Robert E. Lee and Jefferson Davis, as well as First Lady Mary Todd Lincoln. Lizzy and Mary grew to become close friends and confidantes—especially after the assassination of President Abraham Lincoln in 1865. Lizzy's autobiography was published two years later and documented her extraordinary journey from a Southern plantation to the White House.

VIRGINIA MINOR

1824–1894

One St. Louis woman took groundbreaking steps to assert her rights as an American citizen, and it led her all the way to the US Supreme Court. Virginia and her husband, Francis, were staunch abolitionists from the South, and they moved to St. Louis in the 1840s. Virginia became an active member of the Ladies' Union Aid Society during the Civil War. Following the end of the war and the sudden death of her 14-year-old son, she turned her attention to politics and women's voting rights. In 1867 she organized the Woman Suffrage Association, the first organization in the country devoted solely to the cause.

Along with Francis, who was an attorney, Virginia crafted a revolutionary interpretation of the newly ratified 14th Amendment, which stated in part that "all persons born in the United States . . . are citizens, and no State can [deny] the privileges of citizens." She argued that women were citizens, and one of the privileges of citizenship was the right to vote, meaning that women already had the right–they just had to act on it. After hearing Virginia speak at an 1869 suffrage convention, Susan B. Anthony was inspired to try to vote in 1871, an act of defiance that resulted in her arrest.

Virginia tested her views in 1872 by attempting to register to vote in the presidential election. She was denied. Because women weren't allowed to bring cases to court, Francis filed a suit with the St. Louis Circuit Court on her behalf. After several losses and appeals, the case ended up in front of the US Supreme Court. It unanimously ruled against Virginia in 1874, stating that citizenship alone did not guarantee voting rights. The decision reverberated throughout the national suffrage movement, and the loss was a devastating one. Virginia remained the heart of St. Louis's suffrage movement until her death in 1894. After that the fight for suffrage lost momentum, and it would take another 15 years for suffragists to regroup and begin their fight again.

ANNA BRACKETT

1836–1911

Sometimes an unplanned detour brings an unexpected opportunity. For Anna Brackett, St. Louis was supposed to be a brief stopover on her way home to Massachusetts, but it became the place where she was hired as the country's first woman principal of a normal school–an institution where high school graduates are trained to become teachers. Today the school is called Harris-Stowe State University.

During her nine years in St. Louis, Anna began a lifelong relationship with Ida Eliot, the vice principal at the normal school and niece of William Greenleaf Eliot, the chancellor of Washington University in St. Louis. When Anna resigned from her position because of changes to the school's curriculum in 1872, she and Ida moved to New York City to establish their own private school for girls. During that time the couple adopted and raised two daughters.

In addition to her work in the classroom, Anna was a noted philosopher and wrote many books and stories about topics from educational philosophy to poetry. She was considered an international authority on women's education; her work was printed in numerous publications, including the *New York Times* and *Harper's Bazaar*; and she was the editor of the *Journal of Education*.

PRISCILLA HENRY

1829–1895

Born into slavery on an Alabama plantation, Priscilla Henry eventually ran one of St. Louis's most successful businesses of the late 1800s—a brothel. After the Civil War ended she moved north to St. Louis and found work, first as a maid at a hotel and then as a laundress at a brothel on Lucas Avenue. After the social evil ordinance was passed in July 1870 and prostitution was made legal in the city, Priscilla seized the moment and opened her own bordello.

Even after prostitution was outlawed for good in 1874, Priscilla continued to operate two highly profitable "bawdy houses" on 6th Street for another two decades. Segregation laws forbade white and Black women from working together, so Priscilla maintained the brothels side by side. They were opulent buildings with furnishings that were just as luxurious as those found in the city's wealthiest residences.

Although Priscilla couldn't read or write, she earned a fortune estimated at $100,000—equivalent to about $2 million today. At one point she purchased the Alabama plantation where she was born. Priscilla was known as an honest, fair, and discreet madam, and she gained the respect of the police and the powerful men who frequented her establishments. When she died in 1895, newspapers from New York City to Denver noted her passing. Thousands of mourners walked in the streets for Priscilla's funeral procession, and others stood outside her brothels for a moment of silence.

EDUCATOR

ANNA SNEED CAIRNS

1841–1930

Lacking substantial funding, furniture, and equipment, Anna Sneed Cairns opened Kirkwood Seminary, a school for girls, in November 1861, when she was just 20 years old. Bold and seemingly fearless, she regularly took on monumental challenges–and usually succeeded.

Anna Sneed graduated at 17 from Monticello Female Seminary in Godfrey, Illinois, and decided to become a teacher. The daughter of a Presbyterian minister, she was deeply religious and left St. Louis after public-school administrators refused to let her teach the Bible in the classroom. She returned to her hometown when the Civil War began and started developing plans for Kirkwood Seminary.

Her school flourished, but after conflicts with the Kirkwood government she sold the property to a group of wealthy African Americans, who turned the campus into a training school. Kirkwood officials were not happy with her decision–they wanted to push Black people out of the community, not welcome them in. Meanwhile, Anna and her husband, architect John Cairns, purchased property south of Forest Park, where they designed and built Forest Park University. The school opened in 1891 and ran for 35 years. Anna sold the school in 1926 but remained an outspoken advocate for suffrage, prohibition, prison reform, and women's education until her death in 1930.

FANNY WOODWARD

1837–1916

For working parents, the quality and affordability of childcare can lead either to greater family stability or to financial disaster. Thanks to the early leadership of Fanny Woodward, South Side Day Nursery has filled this critical need for families for more than 130 years.

In 1886, Fanny and a group of St. Louis women developed plans for a day nursery that would be the first of its kind west of the Mississippi. Just six weeks later South Side opened its doors. A wife and mother of three daughters, Fanny became South Side Day Nursery's first director in 1887. Under her leadership the nursery expanded its services, adding a kindergarten as well as after-school care for older children. To reach as many families as possible, South Side advertised in pamphlets printed in German, Bohemian (Czech), and English. For 5 cents a day each child received a bath, clean clothes, and three meals. By its second year in operation the nursery had served nearly 5,000 children.

As its president for 20 years, Fanny built a solid foundation that endures to this day. Now known as SouthSide Early Childhood Center, it is still an active part of the St. Louis community and cares for nearly 200 children every year.

EMMA L. WARR

ca. 1850–1937

Being a patient at St. Louis's City Hospital wasn't for the faint of heart. There were no trained nurses on staff, and patients were responsible for measuring and taking their own medications. Bedbugs, rats, and roaches were regular sights, and a single security guard served as the entire night staff. All of that changed when Emma L. Warr arrived in 1884.

A native of Brooklyn, New York, she was educated at the New York Hospital Training School for Nurses and later appointed as the first superintendent of the new St. Louis Training School for Nurses. Part of the infamous City Hospital, it was the only professional nursing school in Missouri.

Alarmed by City Hospital's conditions, Emma quickly arranged for her students to take over most of its nursing care. She added 80 hours of physician lectures and extensive classroom training, lengthening the nursing program from two to three years. By the time Emma retired in 1909, more than 200 women had graduated from her esteemed school. She also pushed for state laws that would recognize and license nurses as medical professionals.

EDUCATOR

SUSAN BLOW

1843–1916

More than 4 million American children attend kindergarten each year, but in 1870 most people didn't even know what the word "kindergarten" meant. When the Des Peres School opened in 1873, it was the first public kindergarten in the country. For Susan Blow, it was the culmination of years of study and planning.

Born in 1843, Susan was the oldest of six children. As part of a prominent St. Louis family committed to education, she attended private schools in New Orleans and New York City, where she was a bright and inquisitive student. While traveling through Germany with her father, Susan was inspired by the educational philosophy of Friedrich Froebel and came to believe that young children learned best by playing and exploring, not by memorizing facts.

When she returned to St. Louis in 1873, she convinced the city's public school superintendent to let her open a kindergarten in her Carondelet neighborhood. She taught 42 students during her first year, and the next year she opened a school to train kindergarten teachers. Within five years there were more than 50 kindergartens in St. Louis, all of them created by Susan. An illness forced her to retire early, but she continued to write and speak about the values of early childhood "learning through play" until her death in 1916.

KATE CHOPIN

1850–1904

Activism doesn't always come with picket signs and marches. Sometimes it comes in the form of a well-written novel published decades before it could be fully appreciated. Kate Chopin's *The Awakening*, first released in 1899, explores ideas about female freedom in the story of a young wife and mother who comes to a tragic end. Beyond a few lukewarm reviews, the book was largely condemned for its depiction of interracial marriage and frank portrayal of female sexuality. For 50 years it was out of print and largely forgotten, only to be rediscovered in the 1950s.

Kate Chopin was born into a wealthy St. Louis family, educated in Catholic schools, and married at 19. After her father was killed in a railroad accident, she was raised by strong, educated women, including her mother and grandmother. From an early age Kate spent time thinking about what it meant for a woman to be free; these thoughts were complicated, as her family were enslavers who supported the Confederacy.

A voracious reader, she kept a journal and wrote short stories. Her husband, Oscar, respected her as an intellectual equal and encouraged her writing, but it wasn't until after his death that she seriously considered publishing her work. Unfortunately, the public's response to *The Awakening* essentially ruined her reputation as a writer. In 1904, after spending the day at the St. Louis World's Fair, she collapsed from a cerebral hemorrhage and died two days later, never knowing that her novel would go on to be a celebrated example of early feminist literature.

MARY HANCOCK MCLEAN

1861–1930

An enthusiastic advocate for women's health, Mary Hancock McLean was one of the first formally trained female physicians to practice in St. Louis. Born in Washington, Missouri, Mary was tutored privately and began studying at Lindenwood College when she was just 13 years old. She graduated from the University of Michigan's medical school in 1883, then moved back to her home state.

With limited employment options, she joined the staff of the St. Louis Female Hospital, which treated poor women and prostitutes. She opened her own practice in 1885, specializing in obstetrics and gynecology. Her first patient, a Black woman named Tillie, needed surgery for a uterine fibroid. Mary spent days sterilizing her instruments before performing the operation in Tillie's home. News of the surgery's success traveled quickly, and Mary was soon one of the city's most in-demand doctors.

That same year, Mary became the first woman member of the St. Louis Medical Society. She was purportedly nominated for membership as "M. H. McLean" to hide that the *M* stood for *Mary*. It took nearly two decades for the society to admit another female physician. She opened the Evening Dispensary for Women in 1893, a clinic that provided free and affordable medical services for working women until 1928. Mary was deeply religious and took several medical mission trips to Asia, where she paid for the medical training of several Chinese and Japanese women.

CHARLOTTE RUMBOLD

1869–1960

Perhaps it was Charlotte Rumbold's five-foot stature that led people to underestimate her power and tenacity. Born and raised in the affluent West End neighborhood, Charlotte pursued a career in social work, devoting her time and seemingly endless energy to helping the poor.

By 1900, Charlotte had turned her attention to city reform. Disturbed by what she witnessed in St. Louis's slums, she began establishing playgrounds as a way to improve children's health. She also joined the Civic League of St. Louis, a group dedicated to revamping the city's infrastructure. Charlotte kept health and recreation at the forefront of her efforts and pushed for the construction of city-run public bathhouses and playgrounds.

Charlotte was appointed to a salaried position in St. Louis's parks department in 1907 while continuing to volunteer with the Wednesday Club and the Civic League. That same year she authored a groundbreaking report on the appalling conditions of the city's worst neighborhoods. As Charlotte's responsibilities with the parks department expanded, she asked for a salary increase–from $1,800 to $2,400 per year–but her request was denied by the St. Louis Board of Aldermen. She resigned from her position in 1916 and moved to Cleveland, where she continued to work in city reform.

S. LOUISE MARSH

1867–1946

How do you change a law when you don't have the right to vote or a voice in the political process? For Webster Groves resident S. Louise Marsh, the answer was to convince a legislator to write a new law.

An active club woman and mother of two, Louise was horrified when she heard about a 15-year-old girl who lived in a St. Louis orphanage and was forced to turn over her hard-earned wages to her alcoholic father. Under the state's sole guardianship laws, fathers retained total control over their children, including the right to sell them. Mothers had no legal rights at all.

Louise convinced legislator and labor lawyer Alroy Phillips to draft and present a joint guardianship law to the Missouri Senate. Along with written pledges of support from more than 6,000 members of Missouri's Daughters of the American Revolution, it quickly passed through both houses of the state legisture and took effect in March 1913. The new law, popularly known as the Marsh Joint Guardianship Law, granted equal rights to both parents and ensured that Missouri mothers would have an equal say in decisions regarding their children.

FANNIE SELLINS

1872–1919

Although Fannie Sellins is remembered as one of the nation's most revered union activists, she began her career as a garment worker in St. Louis. Fannie moved to the city after she married, but her husband died young, leaving her a widowed mother of four. She found work in a garment factory and discovered awful conditions, such as being locked into the facility each morning.

Determined to improve the treatment of workers, Fannie was instrumental in organizing Local #67 of the International Ladies' Garment Workers' Union and soon became its chief negotiator. During a major strike in 1911, she represented more than 400 workers and demanded a 9-hour workday–instead of the required 14-hour day–as well as wage increases.

Her successful negotiation in St. Louis made national news, and in 1913 she moved to West Virginia to support the United Mine Workers of America and their families. In 1919 she continued her work in Pennsylvania. Beloved by union workers, she was also a target of anti-unionists and was arrested many times. Fannie was murdered at 47 years old during a violent strike in Pennsylvania.

ANNIE TURNBO MALONE

1869–1957

When Annie Turnbo Malone came to St. Louis in 1902 hoping to expand her small cosmetics business, few would have guessed that she'd become one of the richest women in the world. Two years earlier she'd invented Wonderful Hair Grower, the first of what would develop into a complete line of beauty products for African American women. Initially Annie and a few assistants sold Wonderful Hair Grower door-to-door, but she soon brought other women into the business, training them as franchised saleswomen. By 1918 Annie was a multimillionaire, and her company, Poro, employed 75,000 women worldwide.

A generous philanthropist, Annie gave money to local organizations and to historically Black colleges across the country. For nearly 25 years she was the president of the St. Louis Colored Orphans Home, which was later renamed in her honor. In 1920, Annie built a new training and distribution facility that covered an entire block in the Ville neighborhood. The building, called Poro College, also held a public cafeteria, hotel rooms, and a 500-seat auditorium. Poro College became the Ville's vibrant center, just as she had intended. Annie's business declined following a contentious divorce and costly settlement. Still, she remained an astute businesswoman and dedicated philanthropist until her death in 1957.

CAROLINE THUMMEL

1873–1947

Caroline Thummel, one of Missouri's first practicing women attorneys, fought for prison reform and equal rights for women. She earned a law degree from St. Louis's Benton College of Law and was admitted to the American Bar Association in 1908. Despite being qualified to practice law at the federal level, she wasn't allowed to join the Missouri Bar Association, which refused to allow women into its ranks.

Caroline argued that punishment should be proportionate to a crime's severity. She criticized the state's judicial system for sentencing a man who stole $3,000 to the same prison term as a man who stole 25 cents. After a former prisoner alleged abuse and neglect at the St. Louis Workhouse, she investigated and confirmed the claims–even though mistreatment had been denied by both the warden and the mayor. She berated the judicial and correctional systems for not doing enough to rehabilitate inmates.

A passionate champion of equality, Caroline was criticized for saying that women should be allowed to propose marriage. She believed that if women had a greater voice in their partnerships, the divorce rate would fall and society would be happier.

IRMA ROMBAUER

1877–1962

For nearly a century, millions of Americans have turned to Irma Rombauer's *Joy of Cooking* to help them get dinner on the table. Despite its name, Irma's cookbook was the product of tragedy, financial hardship, and one woman's resolve to provide for her family.

Irma's husband committed suicide in 1930, leaving her with little income and many bills to pay. Although she was known more for her hosting skills than her cooking ones, Irma decided to write a cookbook for herself. She gathered new recipes as well as those that she had used over the years, all of them calling for common ingredients. Her straightforward approach to cooking–including clear instructions, such as "stand facing the stove"–appealed to beginners and seasoned chefs alike. She also listed the dishes' ingredients within the recipe, a simple but important innovation that made the directions even easier to follow.

Using half of her savings, Irma self-published *Joy of Cooking* in 1931, illustrated by her daughter, Marion. The book had an initial print run of 3,000, and many of the first sales came through word of mouth. As the book's popularity grew, the Bobbs–Merrill Company expressed interest in purchasing its rights, and Irma was bullied into signing a contract that limited the money she earned from sales. By 1936 it had become a national sensation and a kitchen staple. Today *Joy of Cooking* is in its ninth edition and has sold more than 18 million copies. The New York Public Library named it one of the 150 most influential books of the 20th century–the only cookbook to be given the honor.

MARGUERITE MARTYN

1878–1948

Amelia Earhart. Theodore Roosevelt. Jane Addams. Jack London. Ginger Rogers. Woodrow Wilson. No one was safe from the pen of Marguerite Martyn. Despite having a shy and unassuming demeanor, Marguerite was a bold journalist and artist for the *St. Louis Post-Dispatch*. At a time when few journalists–let alone women journalists–were credited for their work, she always received a byline. Her stories and sketches frequently appeared on the paper's front page, and they made her a local celebrity.

Holding a degree in art from Washington University in St. Louis, Marguerite was first hired at the *Post-Dispatch* as an illustrator, but an editor convinced her to also try her hand at writing. Even after she proved to be a talented journalist, she continued to see the world through the eyes of an artist, preferring to sketch during interviews rather than take notes. She went on to write and illustrate stories for more than 35 years.

Her drawings were often humorous critiques of high society and national politics that provided a glimpse into St. Louis life in the early 20th century. Although her name has been largely forgotten, her work–including coverage of the suffrage movement–endures as an invaluable record of St. Louis history.

CLUB WOMAN

ARSANIA WILLIAMS

ca. 1875–1954

Known in St. Louis's African American community as "the Human Dynamo," Arsania Williams worked tirelessly to improve the lives of those who crossed her path. A celebrated teacher in St. Louis's segregated public schools for nearly 50 years, she also served as the president of the St. Louis and Missouri chapters of the National Association of Colored Women.

Born in Louisiana and raised in St. Louis, Arsania graduated in 1895 from the teacher training program at Sumner Normal School, the city's only high school for Black students. Besides teaching full time at Dumas Elementary School, Arsania was a founding member of the Phyllis Wheatley YWCA, where she held leadership positions for nearly two decades. Part of her greatest legacy was helping establish clubs throughout the city that were dedicated to the enrichment of African American women and girls.

Arsania also taught Sunday school, volunteered at her church, and was the dean of the Women's Home Missionary Society. While she considered a life of service its own reward, Arsania received numerous honors from local and national institutions before her death in 1954.

MARIE MEYER

1899–1956

For many people in the early 1920s, seeing a plane fly for the first time was a life-changing event. For Marie Meyer, flying became her passion and her livelihood. Not only did she learn to fly, but she also taught herself death-defying stunts that she performed from the wings of her own plane.

As a child Marie spent hours watching the planes overhead at the Forest Park airmail fields, and at 18 she began taking flying lessons. At 21, she was one of the first women to earn a pilot's license and soon bought her own plane. As she flew around Missouri and Illinois giving demonstrations and selling sightseeing trips, Marie discovered that audiences were captivated by stunt flying–particularly when it was done by a woman.

She organized Marie Meyer's Flying Circus in 1924, and for the next five years, her team of pilots and performers entertained people in towns all over the Midwest. One performer, Bertie Brooks, hung from the plane by his teeth without a safety net or harness. Marie herself performed stunts on the wing of a plane flown by her husband, and a young pilot named Charles Lindbergh occasionally took part in her shows.

Marie's performances showcased aviation's limitless possibilities, and she became a legend. But as flying became more common, the public's interest in Marie's shows tapered off. She closed her business and ran a chain of gas stations and a candy store with her husband in Macon, Missouri.

PEARL CURRAN

1883–1937

In 1917, a novel written by a 17th-century woman became a national bestseller. But the manuscript wasn't old–it was brand-new text, communicated through a St. Louis housewife. On July 8, 1913, Pearl Curran and a friend huddled over a Ouija board, just as they had many times before. But this night was different, and a clear message came through: "Many moons ago I lived. Again I come. Patience Worth my name. . . ."

For the next 25 years, Pearl communicated regularly with Patience, the spirit of a 17th-century English woman, who Pearl said conveyed novels and poems to her. Neighbors, friends, and curious strangers soon began visiting Pearl in her home, hoping to hear from Patience. As Pearl's reputation grew, she began publishing Patience's stories in magazines and even secured several book deals. Respected authors lauded her writing, and in 1918 the Joint Committee of Literary Arts of New York named her an outstanding author.

Pearl's claim of communicating with a long-dead woman was met with both doubt and fascination. Skeptics suggested that she was simply a frustrated housewife looking for attention and fame. But Pearl never changed her story and insisted that Patience was real. Regular public demonstrations silenced many doubters. Supporters claim that Pearl, a woman with only a ninth-grade education, could not have produced that quality and volume of literature by herself. Detractors think she invented Patience as a way to express herself and capitalize on the country's obsession with spiritualism and the occult in the early 1900s. Even today the debate–and the intrigue–lives on.

MIRIAM COSTE SENSENEY

1882–1959

Restaurants, groceries, butcher shops, candy stores–no food establishment escaped the critical eye of Miriam Coste Senseney. Although the Pure Food and Drug Act became law in 1906, food safety remained an issue for decades. Miriam took it upon herself to guarantee that St. Louis's restaurants and food production facilities met strict sanitation standards.

Miriam, an active member of the St. Louis branch of the National Consumers League, forged a partnership with the state's food commissioner. Starting in 1912 they teamed up to conduct regular inspections and rate each facility from 0 percent to 100 percent compliant. Businesses that passed inspection were added to the "white list" and were allowed to display the National Consumers League "white label." To increase public awareness, Miriam invited local journalists and photographers to document the inspections.

Many business owners began cleaning and updating their facilities before Miriam's visits, knowing that a bad inspection could ruin their business but a good one could bring in more customers. By 1915, Miriam had amassed a group of 48 women to serve as volunteer city health inspectors. Although her unpaid work went largely unrecognized, it vastly improved food safety all across the city.

I have no riches but my thoughts Yet these are wealth enough for me

SARA TEASDALE

1884–1933

The great poet Sara Teasdale once said her art was fueled by the tensions between her two selves. On the one hand, she was adventurous and curious–she loved to travel and read poems and stories about the beauty of the world. On the other, she battled illness and frailty for her whole life, spending much of her time alone with her thoughts while confined to her room. She also felt torn between her traditional Victorian upbringing and her pursuit of free expression.

Out of these tensions, though, Sara penned some of the most widely acclaimed poetry of the early 20th century. When she was healthy enough to attend school, she went to the Mary Institute and graduated from Hosmer Hall in 1903. She later joined the Potters, an influential group of women artists in St. Louis. Their magazine, the *Potter's Wheel*, published some of her earliest works.

In 1907, Sara published her first collection of poetry, *Sonnets to Duse and Other Poems*. Critics praised its lyricism and its exploration of complicated ideas about beauty, love, and death. In 1916 she moved to New York, where her work attracted even more attention. In 1918, her collection of poems titled *Love Songs* earned high acclaim, and she won an award equivalent to what is now the Pulitzer Prize for Poetry.

But despite all her success, Sara never found peace. In 1933, after years of personal turmoil and illness, she died by suicide. More than a century later, her words continue to resonate.

ARCHITECT

MAY STEINMESCH

1893–1979

"In 1915 there were four girls in the School of Architecture at Washington University. Apprised of the fact there were other women enrolled at other Universities in the same field, we organized. . . ."

May Steinmesch knew that she wanted to become an architect, but the men enrolled in Washington University's architecture program weren't as enthusiastic about her choice. At a time when many women were exploring new career possibilities in a post-Victorian world, not everyone was excited about making room for them in male-dominated fields.

Although she was a gifted student, as a woman, May wasn't allowed to join the student architecture group. In 1915, May and three other women classmates formed their own professional student association they called La Confrérie Alongive. The name, literally "The Association of Alongive," was a nod to 16th-century Italian architect Giacomo Barozzi da Vignola, whose work inspired the group. The four soon discovered that many other American women were looking to join a professional network of women architects. By 1922, the group reorganized as Alpha Alpha Gamma, and chapters opened across the country. May was its first president. In 1948 the organization became the Association of Women in Architecture and Allied Arts (AWA). Now known as AWA+D, the group remains active.

May graduated in 1916 and found work with St. Louis's newly formed City Planning Commission. For several years she worked closely with Harland Bartholomew, the city's first urban planner, to develop a comprehensive city plan. She continued to work for the government and the military for the next two decades, designing facilities with the US Army Corps of Engineers at Scott Air Force Base. During World War II she moved to San Francisco, where she designed buildings for the United Service Organizations.

JULIA DAVIS

1891–1993

In 1974 the St. Louis Public Library did something it had never done before: It named a new branch after a living person. It was a well-deserved honor for Julia Davis. A graduate of St. Louis public schools and Stowe Teachers College, Julia began teaching at the Ville neighborhood's Simmons Elementary in 1913. In a time of segregation, only Black students attended Simmons, but they rarely learned about the cultural and historical contributions of African Americans. Julia was committed to filling that void, and she taught her students about Black achievements during her classes on world and American history. For more than 40 years she integrated the stories of African American men and women into the standard curriculum, giving her students a more complete picture of the past.

Julia's passion for learning about African American history began as a child, when she pored over scrapbooks her father had filled with clippings and photos of accomplished African Americans. She encouraged her own students to discover more information for themselves through resources available in local libraries.

In 1941, Julia began creating annual Black history exhibits at the St. Louis Public Library, and when she retired from teaching in 1961, she donated $2,500 (more than $21,000 today) as well as her collection of African American history books to the library. The Julia Davis Collection now contains more than 3,000 works. Before her death in 1993 at the age of 101, she won many prestigious awards and received an honorary doctorate from the University of Missouri–St. Louis.

GERTY CORI

1896–1957

Although today Gerty Cori is remembered as the first American woman to win a Nobel Prize in science, she had to push her way into a system that considered women to be second-class professionals. Gerty and Carl Cori were born in the same year in the same Czech town. They received the same education, and they both earned medical degrees in 1920–the year they married. Equals in every way, they conducted groundbreaking medical research in the same lab, and they published papers together. In 1922, Carl was offered a professorship in Buffalo, New York, while Gerty received no offers. Instead, she worked as a research assistant and earned one-tenth of Carl's pay.

In 1931 the Coris relocated to work at Washington University in St. Louis, but Gerty was again forced to take a low-paying job as her husband's assistant. However, her aptitude and passion for science weren't dependent upon her title or her salary. She returned to the lab just three days after giving birth to their son in 1936.

After 20 years of conducting research, Gerty was finally recognized for her exceptional work. She was promoted to assistant professor, and in 1947 she and Carl were awarded the Nobel Prize for discovering how the body breaks down sugar to use for energy–a process now known as the Cori cycle. From then until her death in 1957, Gerty received numerous accolades, and prominent scientists flocked to St. Louis to work with her.

DISABILITY ADVOCATE

MARIE MOENTMANN

1900-1974

In the early 1900s workers of all ages were desperate for income. They were usually met with low pay, long hours, and dangerous work environments. Child labor laws were rarely enforced, and machinery usually lacked safety measures. At the age of 15, factory worker Marie Moentmann was involved in a preventable accident that changed her life but didn't slow her down.

Like many other poor children, Marie began working at 14 years old to earn money for her family. Instead of attending school, she spent up to 10 hours a day operating a rotary printing press at the Fulton Bag and Cotton Mill. Less than a year later, she was standing at the press when a bag became caught between the machine's rollers. Both of her arms were pulled in and crushed, and they had to be amputated immediately. Her injuries led to multiple corrective surgeries and lengthy hospital stays. The *St. Louis Post-Dispatch* covered her story, and the public responded with an outpouring of money and sympathy.

Marie sued the Fulton Bag and Cotton Mill for $100,000 and was awarded $21,000. The company was charged with violating child labor laws and fined just $25. In the coming years, Marie was fitted with two prosthetic arms and learned new ways to complete everyday tasks. She used her skills as a saleswoman to create a successful business, and by 1931 she was a manager and part-owner of a refrigerator store. Marie married in 1941 and passed away in 1974.

HARRIET BLAND

1915–1991

Although the 1936 Olympic Games in Berlin were widely referred to as "Hitler's Olympics," for a short time they belonged to the United States, thanks to a young St. Louis sprinter. But Harriet Bland didn't even know if she'd be able to participate until the day of the race.

Harriet qualified to run in the 400-meter relay, but then the US Olympic Committee said it couldn't afford to send her to the Games. She was stranded at a training facility in Rhode Island just days before she was due to leave for Berlin. Harriet needed at least $500 for travel expenses— money she didn't have. The *St. Louis Globe-Democrat* created a fund for her and raised $500 in donations in just 30 hours. By then Harriet had already begun hitchhiking from the East Coast back home to St. Louis, and it took several days for the Olympic Committee to locate her.

When Harriet finally arrived in Berlin, she came down with pleurisy, an inflammation of the lungs. Just two days before the race, she was in so much pain that she couldn't run at all. But Harriet was a fighter. On August 9, 1936, she ran the first leg of the 400-meter relay, keeping neck and neck with the German front-runner. The Germans pulled ahead in the second and third legs but fumbled the baton on their last pass. The Americans overtook them and won, setting a new Olympic record in the process. In 1983, Harriet became the fifth woman inducted into the Missouri Sports Hall of Fame, and she's one of just a handful of Missouri women who have won an Olympic gold medal.

AUDREY KISSEL

1926–2017

One St. Louis woman's story is the stuff that movies are made of–literally. During World War II most of America's male athletes were getting dressed in military rather than sports uniforms. That's when Audrey Kissel and women from across the nation became part of a new American pastime: professional women's baseball. The story of these athletes was immortalized in the 1992 film *A League of Their Own*.

Audrey grew up in St. Louis with several brothers. She played baseball from an early age and was a talented softball player in high school. When the All-American Girls Professional Baseball League formed in 1943, friends encouraged her to try out. Despite skepticism from her family, she did. At 18 years old, Audrey left her hometown to join the Minneapolis Millerettes, one of six teams in the league.

Audrey was given the nickname "Pigtails" and was required to attend charm school as part of her training. She had to look her best for each of the eight games she played every week: She wore a pink skirted uniform with shorts underneath, a belt, and a burgundy cap. The Millerettes opened their season on May 27, 1944, against the Rockford Peaches. The team lost, but Audrey's skill at second base was unmistakable. Despite receiving several injuries–including a spike wound to her knee that required seven stitches–she played in almost every game. The Millerettes ended their season with a disappointing 45–72 record.

The following year the team reorganized as the Fort Wayne Daisies, but Audrey wasn't on the roster. She had asked for a $5 raise to her $75 weekly salary. Her request was denied, so she kept her off-season job as a war plant inspector in St. Louis. She married and raised five children. Although Audrey passed away in 2017, the legacy of the All-American Girls Professional Baseball League lives on in one of the most beloved sports movies of all time.

PEARL MADDOX

ca. 1894–1979

Nearly two decades before lunch-counter sit-ins made national headlines, one St. Louis woman waged her own civil rights battle. As more women sought work during World War II, the unequal treatment of African American women in St. Louis had never been more apparent. Pearl Maddox had had enough, and she set her mind on challenging and changing the status quo.

Most downtown department stores allowed African Americans to shop but wouldn't hire them or let them eat at their lunch counters. In 1944, Pearl organized the Citizens Civil Rights Committee (CCRC), an integrated group of women who used tactics like picketing and sit-ins to fight segregation.

On May 15, 1944, Pearl and four other women, Black and white, took their seats at the lunch counter inside Stix, Baer & Fuller, one of the city's largest department stores. They stayed for hours, but the African American women were never served. The women continued to hold weekly sit-ins for the next three months, expanding their protest to two other large department stores: Famous-Barr and Scruggs-Vandervoort-Barney. On July 8 a group of 55 women, all members of the CCRC, conducted a large sit-in and picketed all three stores. Rather than serve the women, the three lunch counters simply closed for the day.

Pearl and the CCRC held weekly sit-ins at multiple locations for nearly a year. Although change came slowly, she succeeded in gaining the attention of the entire city. Her commitment to nonviolent protests to dismantle segregation served as the model for future civil rights action in St. Louis.

WILLIE MAE FORD SMITH

1904–1994

No one sang gospel quite like Willie Mae Ford Smith. For her, faith and music created miracles. She described her style as "the Christian blues. . . . When something's rubbing me wrong, I sing out my soul to settle me down." She taught her craft to the likes of Mahalia Jackson, Fontella Bass, and Joe May. This mentorship earned her the name "Mother Smith," a title she treasured.

Born in 1904, the seventh of 14 children, Willie Mae used music to communicate her faith. She and three of her sisters created a gospel quartet called the Ford Sisters, and they made their national debut at the 1922 National Baptist Convention. As her sisters married and left the group, Willie Mae struck out on her own and caught the attention of Thomas Dorsey, known as "the Father of Gospel Music." Together, they formed the National Convention of Gospel Choirs and Choruses, where Willie Mae continued to foster new singers.

Despite her national fame and incredible talent, Willie Mae didn't have a recording career of her own until she was in her late sixties. Instead, she devoted her life to her faith. Although she was born and raised a Baptist, she later joined the Apostolic Church and became an ordained minister. She was forbidden from preaching from the pulpit, so instead she spoke during her performances, giving "sermonettes"–a practice still used today in gospel music. Willie Mae died in 1994, but her legacy lives on in the music she created and the hundreds of musicians she influenced.

MARTHA GELLHORN

1908–1998

On D-Day, 160,000 soldiers fought their way across Omaha Beach in Normandy, France. But only one woman–Martha Gellhorn–experienced the terror firsthand. Months later, she was one of the first journalists to enter the liberated Dachau concentration camp. At a time when war reporting was the domain of men and often consisted of detailing military strategy, Martha was writing stories that were intensely personal.

Born into a progressive, socially active family in St. Louis, Martha followed in her mother Edna's footsteps and attended Bryn Mawr College. Eager to begin her career as a journalist, she dropped out before graduating. She moved to Paris but returned to the US to work for the Federal Emergency Relief Administration. At the height of the Depression she traveled through the South, coming face-to-face with staggering poverty. She interviewed the people who lived there and wrote about their lives.

With her assignment completed, Martha turned her attention to world affairs. Her first taste of war reporting came during the Spanish Civil War. Covering the war gave her insight into the impending war in Europe, and she was determined to be part of the action. On D-Day she stowed away on a hospital ship and wrote her reports from the beach while wearing a nurse's uniform.

She continued to risk her life and report from the front lines of conflicts all over the world. Although Martha is perhaps best known as Ernest Hemingway's third wife, she was never defined by her relationships. Rather, she found purpose in sharing reality as she found it.

ETHEL SHELLEY

1905–1983

For Ethel Shelley, it took the help of the US Supreme Court to realize her dream of home ownership. After moving to St. Louis in the early 1940s, Ethel and her husband, J. D., worked hard to save enough money to buy a home. Most apartments were too small to comfortably house the couple and their six children. After saving nearly $6,000, the Shelleys had to overcome another obstacle: St. Louis's restrictive housing covenants. These legal agreements required home owners to sell their property exclusively to white buyers. Covenants had been common in many neighborhoods since 1911, and they severely limited housing options for African Americans.

Ethel met with a leader of their church who was also a real estate agent, and he found what seemed to be the perfect solution: a two-family house at 4600 Labadie Avenue. But Ethel and J. D. didn't know that previous owners had put a restrictive covenant in the home's deed, which stated that the home could never be sold to "persons of the Negro or Mongolian race." After the Shelleys moved in, longtime neighbors Fern and Louis Kraemer showed up at their door, informing them that they were being sued for violating the covenant. From then on, Ethel feared her family would be evicted simply because of the color of their skin.

The Missouri Supreme Court ruled for the Kraemers, so the Shelleys took their case to the US Supreme Court. The highest court in the land overruled the Missouri verdict in 1948 by a 6–0 vote. It stated that restrictive covenants violated the 14th Amendment, which granted African Americans equal protection under the law. The house on Labadie stands today as a reminder of one woman's strength and determination to raise a family in a home of her own.

JOSEPHINE BAKER

1906–1975

Josephine Baker spent her life pushing boundaries and breaking barriers, both on and off the stage. A natural performer since childhood, she danced on the streets of East St. Louis to earn money for her poverty-stricken family. By eight years old she was working as a live-in maid, where she was horribly mistreated by her employer, a wealthy white woman. She ran away from home at 15, joined a theatre troupe, and became a popular vaudeville performer. After working in New York City, Josephine moved to the place she would eventually call home: Paris. During that time she debuted *Danse Sauvage*, a show that celebrated Black culture in front of primarily white audiences. She opened her own nightclub in 1926 and continued to gain worldwide fame.

During World War II, Josephine used her performances to gather and share military secrets with the French army. When she overheard German soldiers talking during her shows, she wrote down the information in invisible ink and passed it to the French government.

Despite becoming a French citizen in 1937, Josephine still felt a connection to the United States. She returned to her home country several times in the 1960s and publicly condemned the racism that she encountered. Committed to overcoming racial injustice, Josephine refused to perform for segregated audiences. She was one of only a few women who spoke at the landmark 1963 civil rights march in Washington, DC, and she remained a performer and activist until her death in 1975.

VIRGINIA IRWIN

1908–1980

Only one American woman witnessed the final fall of Berlin from inside its borders in 1945. Three days before Adolf Hitler committed suicide, journalist Virginia Irwin traveled 80 miles to the city, where Hitler was holed up in his bunker. Berlin was at the center of Nazi operations and had been closed to foreign journalists since 1941. But for Virginia, the trip–at night, without permission, and without a map–was worth the risk.

Virginia had spent years as a reporter waiting for her big break. Born in Quincy, Illinois, she attended Lindenwood College and found work in the early 1930s as a file clerk at the *St. Louis Post-Dispatch*. Eventually she began writing, but she was restricted to "female" topics, such as food and shopping. After the bombing at Pearl Harbor, Virginia was determined to find a way to cover World War II from the front lines. The *Post-Dispatch* denied her request, so she took a leave of absence and joined the Red Cross as a writer stationed in England. She sent stories to the *Post-Dispatch* editors anyway, and they began printing them. Eventually, they gave her credentials as a correspondent, and she joined up with several active army units.

Months later, she and two companions secretly journeyed over unmarked roads toward Berlin–still occupied by the Nazis, who were fighting a losing battle against Russian troops. She wrote by candlelight, reporting the incredible things she experienced. The army was angered by her disregard of the rules, which required journalists to obtain official permission before traveling. As a result, her stories were held for over a week, and she was stripped of her press credentials. When she arrived home her editor, Joseph Pulitzer, was so impressed with her work that he paid her an additional year's salary.

JEAN ROUVEROL

1916–2017

One evening in January 1951, two uniformed agents from the House Un-American Activities Committee knocked on Jean Rouverol's front door, changing her life forever. Like many of their fellow Hollywood writers and actors during World War II, Jean and her husband, Hugo Butler, had joined the American Communist Party in the 1940s. At the time the United States and the Soviet Union were allies in the fight against Adolf Hitler and the Third Reich, and communism was tolerated–if not outright accepted–in America. But by 1951 the US and the Soviet Union were on opposite sides of the Cold War, and Americans with communist leanings faced jail time.

Jean had been part of the Hollywood community since the 1930s, acting in films with W. C. Fields, Katharine Hepburn, and Gene Autry, before turning her attention to writing novellas and screenplays. Despite her popularity, Jean feared that she may be imprisoned for her political views, just as many of her friends had been. To keep their growing family together, Jean and Hugo moved to Mexico for the next 13 years. Jean continued to write in Mexico but was blacklisted in Hollywood. The US government labeled Jean a "subversive and dangerous revolutionary," and no studio would read her work. But she continued to earn a living by submitting her screenplays under a false name and by using friends who claimed the work as their own. *Autumn Leaves*, a screenplay she co-wrote with Hugo during their time in Mexico, became a film starring Joan Crawford.

The Rouverols were finally able to return to the United States in 1964. When Hugo died in 1968, Jean became an award-winning soap opera writer and taught up-and-coming writers. In 2017 she passed away at the age of 100.

KATHERINE DUNHAM

1909–2006

"So many times, people tell you what you can't do. I don't think about those things. I think mostly about what I can do and what needs to be done." By the end of her life, Katherine Dunham had proven that there were few things she couldn't do. Best known as a dancer and choreographer, Katherine also completed her doctorate in anthropology at the University of Chicago, and she was a professor and an author. She combined her fascination with the human experience across different cultures with her passion for dance to create a groundbreaking new form of expression known as the Dunham Technique, a method still widely practiced today. Katherine fused Afro-Caribbean dance with classical ballet–and in so doing, changed the world of modern dance.

Dunham dancers don't learn just dance. They also learn language, culture, and history. Katherine believed that dance is a reflection of "the meaning of your life, the meaning of the people you came from, your family, and your roots." She brought these ideas to East St. Louis, where she opened the Performing Arts Training Center in the 1960s. Her choreographed pieces shared the African American experience with integrated audiences across the country and around the world.

Katherine used her work and celebrity for activism. She refused to perform for segregated audiences, and through her ballet *Southland*, she exposed the horror of lynching. When she was in her eighties she went on a 47-day hunger strike to bring attention to the plight of Haitians. Though Katherine accomplished much in her life, she said she wanted her epitaph to read not "She did it," but "She tried."

FRANKIE MUSE FREEMAN

1916–2018

Few civil rights activists in American history have had the ear of the president and the power to create national law. A native of Virginia, Frankie Muse Freeman graduated from Howard University School of Law in 1947, then moved with her husband and two young children to St. Louis. She contacted dozens of local law firms for a job, but none would hire her. Instead, she opened her own practice and partnered with the National Association for the Advancement of Colored People (NAACP) to take on discrimination issues.

In 1952 she led the NAACP legal team that filed a class-action suit against the St. Louis Housing Authority. Two apartment complexes were being built, and the city had decided that white residents would live in one and Black residents would live in the other. The judge sided with Frankie, ruling that race could not be a factor in determining who lived in which building. That lawsuit ended segregated public housing in St. Louis.

Leaders of the St. Louis Housing Authority were impressed with her litigation skills, and they hired her as their general counsel, a position she held for the next 15 years. Her work fighting discrimination didn't go unnoticed. In 1963, Frankie met with President John F. Kennedy, and in 1964 she was appointed as the first woman—and the only Black member—of the US Commission on Civil Rights, on which she served until 1980. Frankie returned to St. Louis in 1982, where she continued to work in law and served as a prominent leader in the civil rights movement until her death in 2018.

ROSE CHURCH

1922–2012

The world held its breath as the first generation of American astronauts prepared for their inaugural mission into uncharted territory. But before these men could get to space, they first had to get by St. Louisan Rose Church. In 1959, Rose became the nation's first aerospace nurse and provided groundbreaking care for the team training to fly in the first mission of the US space program.

Rose was hired at McDonnell Aircraft as an industrial nurse in 1951. At that time the company was manufacturing fighter planes, but in 1959 it won the contract to build the *Mercury* capsule, which was to be America's first manned space vehicle. When the company advertised for an aerospace physician, Rose made her move, telling president James S. McDonnell that the team would also need a nurse. She got the job. For the next eight years Rose monitored and cared for America's first astronauts as they trained for their missions, including the Gemini project. She was among the first on the scene in 1966 when a training exercise at Lambert Airport resulted in the death of two astronauts.

For most Americans, Alan Shepard, Dick Gordon, Jim Lovell, John Glenn, and Neil Armstrong were larger-than-life pioneers, legends in their own time. For Rose, these men were her patients—and her friends. After leaving McDonnell Aircraft in 1967, she regularly spoke about her experiences as the nation's first aerospace nurse and remained an enthusiastic supporter of the US space program until her death in 2012.

MARGARET BUSH WILSON

1919–2009

A pioneering civil rights lawyer, Margaret Bush Wilson spent a lifetime proving that racial and gender barriers were made to be broken. After graduating from Lincoln University School of Law in 1943, Margaret became the second African American woman admitted to the Missouri Bar. Over the next two decades she would fight against housing segregation and unfair hiring practices, run for Congress, serve as Missouri's assistant attorney general, and become president of the Missouri chapter of the National Association for the Advancement of Colored People (NAACP).

Margaret's father owned a real estate firm, and he called on her for help as he began untangling the legal issues surrounding the home that he had helped J. D. and Ethel Shelley purchase. She served on the team that took *Shelley v. Kraemer* to the US Supreme Court and ended racial covenants that perpetuated segregated housing. When civil rights activists in St. Louis protested Jefferson Bank's discriminatory hiring practices, many were arrested. Margaret served as their legal counsel.

Both of Margaret's parents were longtime members of the NAACP. She followed in their footsteps and quickly rose through the leadership ranks. In 1962 she became the Missouri branch president and in 1975 was the first woman to serve as the national organization's board chair. Although a falling-out with the NAACP's executive director ended her nine-year tenure, Margaret went on to serve on many university and corporate boards across the country, and she continued to practice law well into her eighties.

FONTELLA BASS

1940–2012

If you turned on the radio in 1965, chances are good that you would have heard Fontella Bass's soulful voice singing her hit song, "Rescue Me." But it took a lead singer who was running late to pull Fontella from behind the piano to center stage.

Born and raised in St. Louis, the Soldan High School graduate began playing the piano at funerals when she was five years old. By the time she was nine, she was touring with her mother, gospel singer Martha Bass. Fontella was the piano player for Little Milton, a popular blues singer, and one night he was late for a show. Fontella stepped up to take his place, and her singing career was born. Soon she was one of Little Milton's featured singers, and she joined the Oliver Sain Soul Revue.

Fontella began recording solo records in 1962, but the songs failed to make much of an impact. It wasn't until she released a duet with Bobby McClure in early 1965 that she gained worldwide fame. After an informal jam session and only three takes, she recorded what would become her best-selling song. Released on September 4, 1965, "Rescue Me" climbed to No. 1 on the R&B charts and made it to No. 9 on the Hot 100. But Fontella was not credited as a songwriter, and she spent years fighting for recognition and royalty rights. Undaunted, she continued recording music through the 1980s.

HARRIETT WOODS

1927–2007

Not many politicians get their start because of a loose manhole cover. In the early 1960s, Harriett Woods was a suburban housewife raising three young sons in University City. But when cars drove over an improperly secured manhole cover in front of her house, the noise woke up her kids from their naps. She asked the city government to fix it; they refused. So Harriett created her own petition on a yellow legal pad, gathered neighbors' signatures, and presented it to those same officials. This time they listened and fixed the cover.

Her success led her to explore other ways of influencing her community, and by 1967 she was appointed to the city council and then to the state's highway commission. In 1976 she ran for the Missouri Senate and won. She was one of few women to hold a legislative office and was often ostracized, but she remained committed to fighting for women's issues, including equal pay and reproductive rights.

The slogan for her 1982 Senate campaign was "Give them hell, Harriett." She was the only woman in America to run for the Senate that year, and she beat out 10 opponents to earn the Democratic nomination. On Election Day she was edged out by incumbent John C. Danforth by less than 2 percent of the vote.

Never one to give up, Harriett was elected lieutenant governor in 1984—the first woman ever elected to a statewide office in Missouri. During her term she focused on helping the elderly, the poor, and the homeless. In the years that followed, Harriett called for more women to become involved in politics. As president of the National Women's Political Caucus, she was a mentor and advocate for many women entering government.

POET

MAYA ANGELOU

1928–2014

Triumph over adversity looks different for everyone. For Maya Angelou, writing was the path to finding the strength she needed to overcome a traumatic childhood. Born in St. Louis in 1928, Maya moved to Arkansas at three years old after her parents divorced. She was raised by her grandmother but continued to visit her mother in St. Louis. One of those visits changed the course of her life. At the age of eight, Maya was raped by one of her mother's friends. Soon after, her uncles killed the man responsible. Maya, having told her mother the man's name, blamed herself for his death and refused to speak for the next five years.

It took another 30 years and the publication of her first autobiographical novel, *I Know Why the Caged Bird Sings*, before Maya found her voice and shared her horrific story with the world. The award-winning book has been a regular target of censorship because of its unflinching depiction of Maya's experiences as a young African American woman in the segregated South.

Maya was also active in the civil rights movement and a friend of Martin Luther King Jr. She produced, directed, and acted in many television programs and stage productions. President Bill Clinton commissioned her to write and read a poem–"On the Pulse of Morning"–at his 1993 inauguration. Her legacy of courage and hope lives on in the words she spoke that day: "Lift up your hearts; Each new hour holds new chances for new beginnings."

INDEX

Angelou, Maya, 102
Anthony, Susan B., 23
Aramepinchieue, 5
Awakening, The, 37
Baker, Josephine, 85
Bass, Fontella, 78, 98
Bland, Harriet, 72
Blow, Susan, 35
Brackett, Anna, 24
Cairns, Anna Sneed, 28
Chopin, Kate, 37
Chouteau, Marie Thérèse Bourgeois, 6
Church, Rose, 95
Citizens Civil Rights Committee (CCRC), 77
Clamorgan, Jacques, 9
Colored Ladies Soldiers' Aid Society, 15
Cori, Gerty, 68
Curran, Pearl, 58
Davis, Julia, 67
Des Peres School, 35
Dunham, Katherine, 91
Duchesne, St. Rose Phillipine, 12
Eliot, Ida, 24
Esther, 9
Freeman, Frankie Muse, 93
Gellhorn, Martha, 80
Henry, Priscilla, 27
Irwin, Virginia, 86
Joy of Cooking, 51
Keckly, Elizabeth, 21
Kissel, Audrey, 74
Laclède, Pierre, 6
Maddox, Pearl, 77

Malone, Annie Turnbo, 47
Marsh, S. Louise, 43
Martyn, Marguerite, 53
McLean, Mary Hancock, 39
Meachum, Mary, 15
Meyer, Marie, 56
Minor, Virginia, 23
Moentmann, Marie, 71
19th Amendment, 3
Parsons, Emily, 19
Performing Arts Training Center, 91
Poro College, 47
Rombauer, Irma, 51
Rouensa, Marie, 5
Rouverol, Jean, 89
Rumbold, Charlotte, 40
Scott, Dred, 16
Scott, Harriet, 16
Sellins, Fannie, 44
Senseney, Miriam Coste, 60
Shelley, Ethel, 82, 96
Smith, Willie Mae Ford, 78
Steinmesch, May, 64
Teasdale, Sara, 63
Thummel, Caroline, 49
Von Phul, Anna Maria, 11
Warr, Emma L., 33
Williams, Arsania, 55
Wilson, Margaret Bush, 96
Woman Suffrage Association, 23
Woods, Harriett, 101
Woodward, Fanny, 30
Worth, Patience, 58